Pebble®
Plus

Look Inside

Look Inside a Pueblo

by Jenny Moss

Consulting Editor: Gail Saunders-Smith, PhD

Consultant:
Ross Frank
Associate Professor, Department of Ethnic Studies
University of California, San Diego

CAPSTONE PRESS
a capstone imprint

Pebble Plus is published by Capstone Press,
151 Good Counsel Drive, P.O. Box 669, Mankato, Minnesota 56002.
www.capstonepress.com

092009
005618CGS10

 Books published by Capstone Press are manufactured with paper containing at least 10 percent
post-consumer waste.

Library of Congress Cataloging-in-Publication Data
Moss, Jenny, 1958–
    Look inside a pueblo / by Jenny Moss.
    p. cm. — (Pebble plus. Look inside)
    Includes bibliographical references and index.
    Summary: "Simple text and photographs present pueblos, including their construction, history, and interaction
with the environment" — Provided by publisher.
    ISBN 978-1-4296-3986-6 (library binding)
    1. Pueblos — Juvenile literature. 2. Pueblo Indians — Juvenile literature. 3. Pueblo architecture — Juvenile
literature. I. Title.
E99.P9M875 2010
978.9004'974 — dc22   2009023389

Editorial Credits
Gillia Olson, editor; Kyle Grenz, designer; Wanda Winch, media researcher; Eric Manske, production specialist

Photo Credits
Alamy/Chuck Place, 19; David South, 21
CORBIS/Michael Freeman, 11
Nativestock.com/Marilyn Angel Wynn, 15
North Wind Picture Archives, 13, 17
Shutterstock/Damian P. Gadal, 9; Duncan Gilbert, 7; George Burba, 5; John S. Sfondilias, back cover, 3; Michelle
    Dulieu, cover; microstocker, 1, 22–23

Note to Parents and Teachers

The Look Inside series supports national social studies standards related to people, places,
and culture. This book describes and illustrates pueblos. The images support early readers
in understanding the text. The repetition of words and phrases helps early readers learn new
words. This book also introduces early readers to subject-specific vocabulary words, which are
defined in the Glossary section. Early readers may need assistance to read some words and to
use the Table of Contents, Glossary, Read More, Internet Sites, and Index sections of the book.

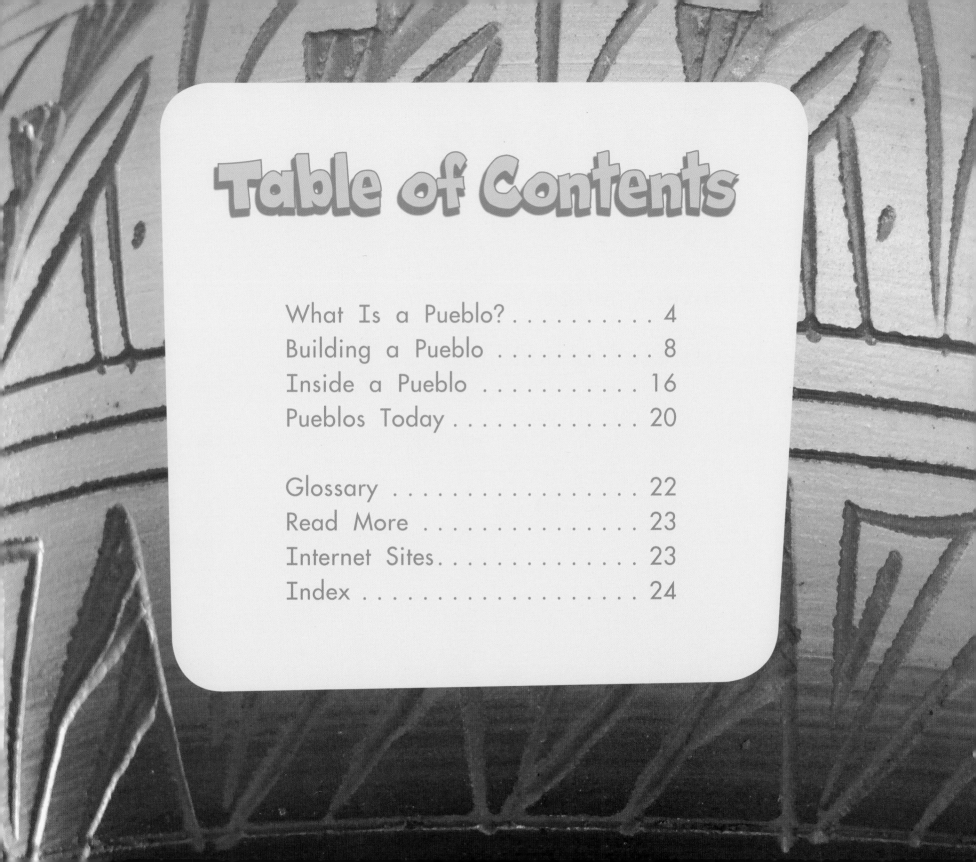

Table of Contents

What Is a Pueblo?

A pueblo is a village

built by Native Americans.

Pueblo homes are big buildings.

Several families may live

in one of these homes.

Ancestors of the Pueblo Indians

built the first pueblos

more than 1,000 years ago.

They lived in the

southwestern United States.

Building a Pueblo

Pueblo homes are made
of stone or adobe.
People make adobe bricks
out of mud and straw.
The bricks dry in the sun.

To build a home's walls,

people stack stone blocks

or adobe bricks.

They use mud to fill cracks.

Roofs are made of wood
with clay packed on top.
They are strong and flat.

Homes have doors in the roofs.

People get to the roof by ladder.

Early pueblo people pulled up

ladders to keep out enemies.

Later homes had doors in walls.

Inside a Pueblo

The inside of a pueblo home is
for sleeping and storing food.
Work is done on the rooftops.

Pueblos have underground
rooms called kivas.
These rooms are sacred places
in the Pueblo religion.

Pueblos Today

Some Pueblo Indians still live in pueblos. These villages are an important part of their way of life.

Glossary

adobe — a brick made of mud and straw that is dried in the sun

ancestor — a family member who lived a long time ago

kiva — an underground room used for religious purposes; the Pueblo Indians built kivas in their villages.

religion — a set of spiritual beliefs that people follow

sacred — very important and deserving great respect; sacred objects are related to a religion.

village — a small town

Read More

Broida, Marian. *The Pueblo*. First Americans. New York: Marshall Cavendish Benchmark, 2006.

Preszler, June. *Pueblos*. Native American Life. Mankato, Minn.: Capstone Press, 2005.

St. Lawrence, Genevieve. *The Pueblo and Their History*. We the People. Minneapolis: Compass Point, 2006.

Internet Sites

FactHound offers a safe, fun way to find Internet sites related to this book. All of the sites on FactHound have been researched by our staff.

Here's all you do:

Visit *www.facthound.com*

FactHound will fetch the best sites for you!

Index

Word Count: 180
Grade: 1
Early-Intervention Level: 16